# Whispers to Krishna

## A Journey of Faith

Saritha Barmala

BookLeaf
Publishing

India | USA | UK

Made with ❤ on the BookLeaf Publishing Platform
www.bookleafpub.in
www.bookleafpub.com

*To Lord Krishna, the eternal source of compassion, guidance, and love. Your divine presence has been my beacon through every challenge and triumph.*

*To all those who feel misunderstood or isolated, may you find solace and strength within these pages. This book is for you, a reminder that even in solitude, you are never truly alone.*

*With deepest gratitude and love,*

# Acknowledgment

First and foremost, I offer my deepest gratitude to Lord Krishna, whose divine presence has been a constant source of strength, guidance, and inspiration throughout my life. Without His infinite compassion and grace, this book would not have been possible.

A special thank you to my editor and the publishing team, whose expertise, dedication, and belief in my vision have brought this book to life. Your hard work and commitment have been instrumental in this journey.

Lastly, I want to express my sincere appreciation to the readers. Your willingness to share in my journey and to explore the depths of faith, love, and forgiveness means more to me than words can express. I hope that this book brings you comfort, inspiration, and a sense of connection to the divine.

With heartfelt gratitude,

# Preface

In the vast tapestry of life, we each have our own unique threads, weaving stories of joy, sorrow, struggle, and redemption. This book is a heartfelt journey into my personal experiences, captured through poems that reflect my innermost thoughts and prayers to Lord Krishna. Through these verses, I share my struggles, longing for love and acceptance, and quest for understanding and forgiveness.

From the tender years of childhood to the complex realities of adulthood, my path has been fraught with challenges that have tested my faith and resilience.

This book is not just a collection of poems but a spiritual odyssey. It explores my relationship with Krishna, my search for inner peace, and my desire to connect with others who may be experiencing similar trials. Through sharing my story, others may find comfort, inspiration, and a sense of solidarity.

# a girl who lived

A girl, just twenty-four, sits in the night,

In her hometown room, where there's no
light.

She's closed every window, locked every door,

No sunlight touches the cold, hard floor.


In the darkness, her tears softly fall,

As she gazes at Krishna on the wall.

His eyes seem distant, his smile so still,

She's searching for answers, against her will.

The room is silent, no sound, no breeze,

Only the weight of her silent pleas.

She's wrapped in shadows, lost in thought,

In this lonely space where comfort is sought.


Her heart feels heavy, her spirit weak,

But in Krishna's image, she dares to seek.

A glimmer of hope in the darkest place,

A silent prayer, a need for grace.


Yet still, she sits, alone in the dark,

With only Krishna to hear her heart.

She started her prayer with a heart, That is Me.

# why lord!

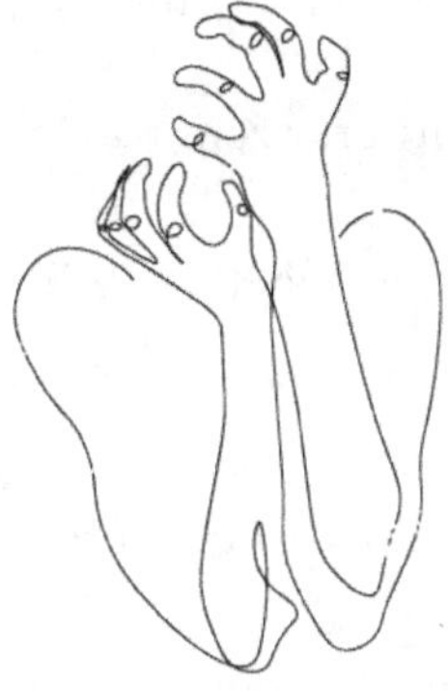

In the quiet of my room, I kneel,

Seeking answers, seeking to heal.

"Krishna," I whisper, "tell me why,

From my father, love passed me by.


Why can't I hold his hand so tight?

Why can't I feel his hug at night?

Why can't I have his kiss so sweet,

Like other girls, when fathers meet?

Why am I the one left behind,

In his heart, why can't I find

The love that others seem to see?

Why does this pain belong to me?


Am I to blame for this cruel fate?

Did sins of past lives seal my state?

# my friend krishna

Oh, Krishna!

My friend is no longer there.

Her loyalty, once firm and true,

Now binds her to someone new.


She inspired me, a guiding light,

But now she's gone, lost from sight.

Why has she drifted far away,

When I need her most, why can't she stay?

Her loyalty, a treasured gift,

Has found another, causing this rift.

In my heart, confusion reigns,

Why this distance, why these pains?


Krishna, hear my silent plea,

Why has this change come to be?

What lesson lies within this sorrow,

To heal my heart for tomorrow?

# my harsh

Krishna, when I speak, it seems like a fight,

My words come out harsh, not soft, not light.

But no, I'm innocent, no harm in my tone,

Just a voice that struggles to stand alone.


It's not anger; it's not rage, you see,

Only the way my heart speaks through me.

There's no complaint, no ill intent,

Just words that sound more than I meant.

My voice is strong, perhaps too loud,

But inside, I'm not so proud.

I'm not fighting; I'm not at war,

Just trying to express what's at my core.


This tone, this peak, is my main flaw,

It hides my gentleness, leaves them in awe.

But Krishna, you know what's deep inside,

A heart that's pure, with nothing to hide.

# my body

When I grew and my body changed,

Mocked and scorned, I felt estranged.

Insults burned, they took their toll,

Isolation claimed my soul.


I pulled away, chose silent ways,

Loneliness filled my days.

Love was scarce, connection thin,

A harsh voice hides the pain within.

Krishna, is this past life's wrong,

That my voice sings a sorrowful song?

Am I to bear this burdened tune,

To pay for sins of life's monsoon?

# darkness

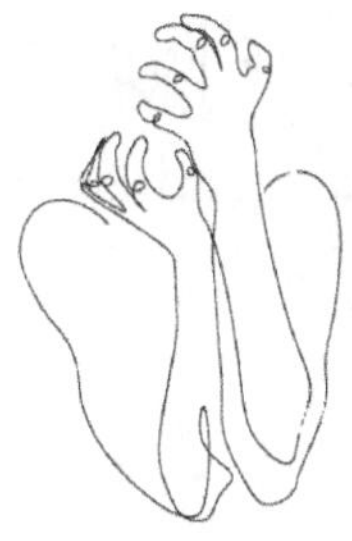

Krishna, in this darkness deep,

I've lost my way; my soul does weep.

Depression's chains, they hold me tight,

Robbing me of joy and light.


Depression's grip, so tight, so strong,

In its hold, I don't belong.

I've lost my path, my sense of glee.


Confidence shattered, studies gone,

While others cheer, their rewards are drawn.

I watch from afar, in silent pain.

Wondering why I've lost my gain.

No interest in love, no joy in play,

Entertainment fades, and dreams decay.

# My sister!

Krishna, why must my heart endure this
weight,

My sister, my rival, shaping my fate?

She is loved by my father, cherished, adored,

While I stand outside, my spirit ignored.


Her beauty's a mask for a selfish heart,

Yet she gathers love, tearing me apart.

Arrogant words fall from her lips,

Yet it's her hand they always grip.

I am her elder, but she gives no respect,

Calls me by name, leaving me wrecked.

Everything I've ever wanted, she's received,

While I'm left behind, deceived.


She's taken all that I hold dear,

And left me with nothing but silent fear.

Depression grows, its darkness spreads,

As I wrestle with these thoughts in my head.

# my destiny?

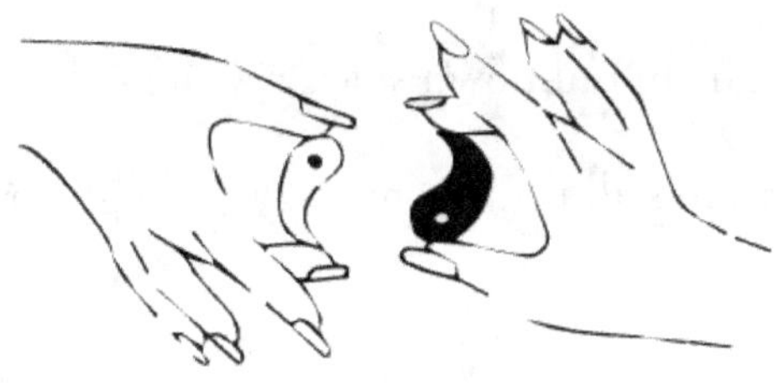

Krishna, the weight on my heart is deep,

At twenty years, my soul can't sleep.

They say it's time; my fate is near,

A marriage arranged, but I'm filled with fear.


How can they decide what's best for me?

A stranger's life, my destiny?

How can they know this path is right,

When my own dreams fade from sight?

I wasn't ready; I wasn't sure,

Yet they insisted, pushed me toward the door.

How can an unknown share my life,

When I'm still finding my way through strife?


I've got goals, big dreams to chase,

A career that I've long embraced.

But how will he, a stranger to me,

Support these dreams that set me free?


Even my family doubts my will,

How can he help my dreams fulfill?

I argued, I resisted, I stood my ground,

But their voices, Krishna, were all around.

# My decision

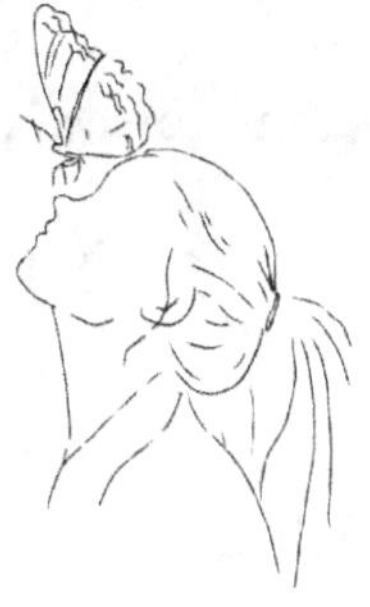

So I made a choice, in silence kept,

A secret vow, and then I wept.

I canceled the wedding, stopped the tide,

But they don't know the truth I hide.


Krishna, the burden still remains,

In my heart, the hidden pains.

They wonder why the wedding ceased,

But only I know of the peace released.

Yes, it was me who stopped the day,

The wedding planned, but not my way.

I took the phone, my voice was clear,

"This isn't my wish; it's driven by fear."


I told him of the dreams I hold,

Of the goals I've set, the future bold.

"I need to study, to grow, to be,

Please understand, this isn't for me."


"Wait for two years, if we're meant to unite,

But right now, my path is in sight."

He listened, then quietly said, "Okay,"

And with those words, the weight gave way.

He cut the call, the silence thick,

But at that moment, I felt a click.

The wedding's off, the chains undone,

I chose my path, and now I run.

# Restart

I restarted my study, picked up my pen,

Revived my career, found strength again.

Stepped into Hyderabad, my dream so near,

With empty pockets, yet no fear.


I walked through streets, unknown and vast,

With hope in my heart, forgetting the past.

In the darkness, a small light shone,

A government hostel, where I wasn't alone.

For people like us, with little to spare,

A place to dream, a place to care.

I began again, with nothing but hope,

In this city of dreams, learning to cope.


So I started to dream, to build, to grow,

In Hyderabad's arms, my ambitions flow.

Though the road is tough, I stand tall,

With dreams in my heart, I'll conquer it all.

# Empty pockets

But Krishna, the struggle was hard to bear,

With empty pockets, I had nothing to spare.

My friends, my roommates, they helped when they could,

But not every time, not like I wished they would.


I needed money for books, for fees,

For the simple things, for basic needs.

I searched the city, desperate and keen,

Until I found a job, a small, hopeful scene.

I was happy then, relief in sight,

But working and studying stole my night.

Balancing both was a heavy strain,

A complicated path, filled with pain.


The job brought money, but the time it took,

Leaving little room for me to look,

At my studies, my goals, my future ahead,

The weight of both, like a stone on my head.


In this dance of work and dreams, I tread,

Wishing for balance, but fear and dread.

The joy of earning, the cost so high,

As I struggled to let my ambitions fly.

# The Pressure

Krishna, the pressure weighed on me so deep,

Both study and job demands that keep.

I was caught in a struggle, tight and tough,

Trying to balance, but it was never enough.


Warnings came from every side,

"Focus more," they said with pride.

But I felt stuck, trapped in the grind,

Helpless, lost, peace I couldn't find.

Somehow I managed, just for a while,

Pushing through with a forced smile.

But the weight grew heavy; I couldn't bear,

So I had to choose, with a heavy heart's care.


I let the job go, released the strain,

Choosing study, though it brought more pain.

Resigned from work; my path was clear,

But the struggle left its mark, severe.

# No Help!

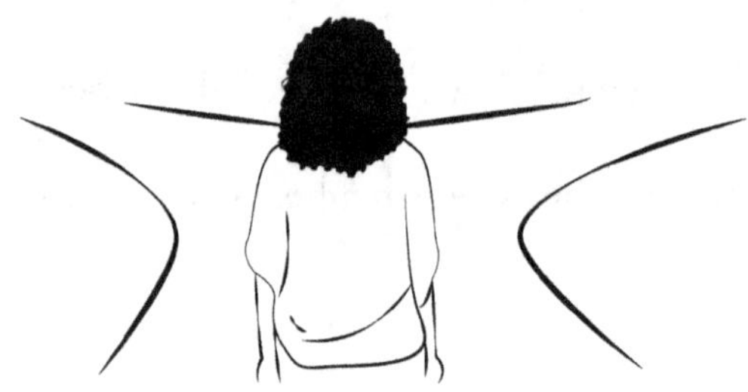

Oh my Lord, the burden's grown so deep,

I managed for five semesters, not a tear to seep.

But then I asked my family, with hope in my voice,

For money to continue, to keep up my choice.


They couldn't help, their pockets bare,

No funds to give, no money to spare.

I cried and cried, lost in despair,

Not knowing what to do, feeling life's unfair.

Fear gripped my heart; tears fell like rain,

I blamed myself, drowning in pain.

This is all my fault, I thought with regret,

For daring to dream, for what I can't forget.


No help in sight, no shoulder to lean,

My dreams now fragile, breaking at the seam.

Oh my Lord, the struggle's too much,

In this harsh world, I've lost my touch.

# I am Lost

Krishna, this is enough; I've reached my end,

I can't struggle anymore; I can't pretend.

I've pushed so hard, but now I break,

I can't move forward; no more can I take.


Stuck in darkness, where no light remains,

I'm drowning in sorrow, wrapped in chains.

So I'm stopping my study, leaving it behind,

Stopping the pain that's clouded my mind.

I admit defeat; I've lost this fight,

A loser in this battle, no strength to ignite.

I'm going home, leaving dreams to fade,

All my hopes, in the air, they've strayed.


Krishna, I'm done; there's nothing left,

Of ambition, of drive, I'm now bereft.

So I walk away, from all I've sought,

In the silence of failure, I'm caught.

# Need Answers

At home, tears fell like endless rain,

Krishna, I'm drowning in this pain.

What must I do to find my way,

To lift this darkness, bring back the day?


I need your guidance, your voice, your light,

To chase away the fears of night.

Relieve me from this heavy strain,

From all this suffering, all this pain.

I long for peace, a mind at rest,

To forget these worries, to feel blessed.

I want to smile, to breathe once more,

To leave this torment on the floor.


Tell me, Krishna, what must I do?

How can I find a path that's true?

I seek your answers, clear and kind,

To bring me peace, to ease my mind.


I want to be happy, free from despair,

To live my life without this care.

Krishna, guide me, show me the way,

Help me find hope, bring back the day.

# I Seek

Krishna, I've never asked for much,

But now I seek your gentle touch.

Why am I failing, where have I gone wrong?

What is it you want from me all along?


Every path I tread seems to fall,

No matter how hard, how much I call.

I've given my all, yet still I lose,

Tell me, Krishna, what must I choose?

What do you see in this heart of mine,

What lesson, what purpose, in this design?

I'm lost in this maze, with no way through,

Krishna, I need answers, I'm asking you.


Why do I stumble at every turn?

What is it you wish for me to learn?

Show me the truth, the reason why,

Why do I keep failing, no matter how I try?


Krishna, I'm pleading; help me see,

What is the path you've set for me?

I never asked for anything before,

But now I seek your wisdom's core.

# No Response

Krishna, I'm pleading, where's your voice?

Why no response, no sign, no choice?

Why does my father withhold his love?

Is there no answer from you above?


Why does my sister show no respect?

Why am I the one she'll always reject?

Why is my voice harsh, so rough, so strange?

Why can't I be sweet, why can't I change?

Why do I keep failing, time and again?

What is the reason for all this pain?

Krishna, I'm lost; I don't understand,

Why these trials, why this heavy hand?


I'm asking, I'm pleading, where's your light?

Why does my path seem void of right?

Why am I not like others I see,

Why must this burden fall on me?

# Why I Didn't

Krishna, tell me, why didn't I stop,

When my father's love fell, a raindrop?

Why didn't I halt when his words cut deep,

When arguments left me with nights I
couldn't sleep?


Why didn't I stop when my sister's scorn
grew,

When her annoyance pierced, and nothing I
could do?

Why didn't I turn away from the pain,

When all I did was meet disdain?

Why didn't I stop when my family withdrew,

When their support faded, and I had no clue?

Why did I keep going, why did I stay,

When they left me alone, day after day?


Why didn't I stop when my friends weren't
there,

When I stood alone, burdened with care?

Why didn't I stop when fate turned its face,

When life's trials put me in this place?


Why did I stand, stubborn and strong,

Holding my ground when all felt wrong?

Why didn't I break, why didn't I bend,

Krishna, why did I choose to defend?

Why did I choose this lonely fight,

When nothing around me seemed right?

Krishna, tell me, why did I stay,

Why didn't I stop and walk away?

# He is in Me

There's no answer, just silence around,

The quiet in my room—not a single sound.

I hear only my heartbeat, my cry so deep,

In this lonely space, where shadows creep.


And then it hits me, clear as day,

This sadness, this weight—it's my own to stay.

I'm the one who holds the key,

But the cause, oh Krishna, it lies in me.

For you are the courage that keeps me strong,

The harsh tone in my voice, where I belong.

You are the faith that anchors my soul,

The light in my eyes that makes me whole.


You're the devil in me, stirring the fire,

The force that pushes me to climb higher.

In every tear, in every fight,

Krishna, you're there, my guiding light.


This sadness, this strength—it's all entwined,

With you in my heart, body, and mind.

I see it now, as clear as can be,

Krishna, you are the force within me.

# The Devil and God

I open the window, gaze at the stone,

In the garden where I stand alone.

Oh, Krishna! You're the devil, the God in me,

Both the shadows and the light I see.


You stop me from paths unknown,

Yet shape me into strength, fully grown.

I feel your power molding my mind,

To face the world, leaving fear behind.

You're teaching me courage, step by step,

Building a warrior with no regret.

I stand now strong, both mind and soul,

Ready to conquer, to reach my goal.


No fear remains, no doubt, no shame,

With you in me, I am never the same.

I can speak my truth, stand tall and proud,

In any crowd, I'm no longer cowed.


You are in me, Krishna, through and through,

The force that drives all I pursue.

Mentally, physically, I've grown so strong,

With you beside me, I can't go wrong.

I face the world with a steady heart,

Knowing we'll never be apart.

For you are the strength, the fire in me,

My guiding light, eternally free.

# He is within You

So this is me now, standing tall,

When problems arise, don't let them make
you fall.

Don't be sad, for there's a reason,

For every challenge, every season.


Everyone enters your life with care,

Each has a purpose, a role to share.

Don't judge; don't rush to decide,

Let time reveal what's hidden inside.

Success may take its time to find,

But never let sadness cloud your mind.

Be strong, hold firm in your place,

Krishna is within; feel his grace.


He will guide you through light and dark,

Have faith, for he's within your heart.

He is you, and you are him,

In every battle, when hope grows dim.


So trust in the journey; let it unfold,

With Krishna within, your spirit bold.

He is the strength in every stride,

With him in you, there's nothing to hide.

www.ingramcontent.com/pod-product-compliance
Lightning Source LLC
Chambersburg PA
CBHW072050150726
47996CB00015B/2464